# Totally Grōss & Awesōme™

# Science

# Facts

## & Jokes

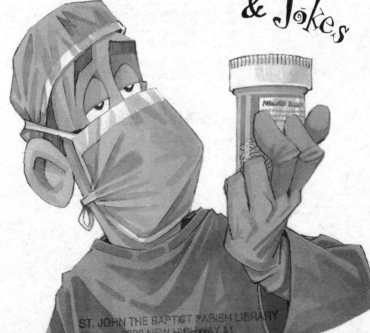

Published in MMXVIII by
Scribo, an imprint of
The Salariya Book Company Ltd
25 Marlborough Place, Brighton BN1 1UB
**www.salariya.com**

ISBN: 978-1-912233-65-6

SALARIYA
SCRIBO   BOOK HOUSE   SCRIBBLERS

1 3 5 7 9 8 6 4 2

A CIP catalogue record for this book is available
from the British Library.

Printed and bound in China.
Printed on paper from sustainable sources.

Created and designed by
David Salariya.

Visit
# www.salariya.com
for our online catalogue and
**free** fun stuff.

PAPER FROM

SUSTAINABLE
**FORESTS**

Author:
**John Townsend** worked as a
secondary school teacher before
becoming a full-time writer.
He specializes in illuminating and
humorous information books for
all ages.

Artist:
**David Antram** studied at
Eastbourne College of Art in
England and then worked in
advertizing before becoming a full-
time artist. He has illustrated many
children's non-fiction books.

# Totally Gross & Awesome™

# Science

# Facts

## & Jokes

This Totally Gross & Awesome
book belongs to:

..............................................

Written by
## John Townsend

Illustrated by
## David Antram

**SCRIBO**
a SALARIYA imprint

# Introduction

Warning—reading this book might not make you LOL (laugh out loud) but it could make you GOL (groan out loud), feel sick out loud, or SEL (scream even louder). If you're reading this in a library by a SILENCE sign... get ready to be thrown out for LOL-GOL-SEL!

The author really hasn't made anything up in this book (apart from some silly limericks and jokes).

He checked out the foul facts as best he could and even double-checked the fouler bits to make absolutely sure—so please don't get too upset if you find out something different or meet a world famous mad scientist/historian/total genius who happens to know better.

If I had my way, I'd RATiFy the lot!

5

# Science Secrets

The word science comes from the Latin "scientia," meaning knowledge. In other words, science is all about trying to find information, answers, and solutions—but be warned… that can take scientists into some gross, yucky, foul, disgusting, and blood-curdlingly cheesy places. By the end of this book, you will be totally grossed out… so here's another warning: don't read this at bedtime—nightmares guaranteed! (Scientifically tested by a team of mad scientists with foulometers.)

# A Quick Guide to Science:

- If it's green or it wiggles, it's biology
- If it stinks, it's chemistry
- If it sparks, it's physics
- If it's very high up, it's astronomy
- If it hurts, it's medical science
- If it makes you feel sick, it's food science
- If it's dead, it's CSI forensic science
- If it crashes and needs rebooting, it's computer science

And they're all in this book!

# Foul Food Science

Science is everywhere—especially in the kitchen. Whenever you cook or eat food, there's a lot of science going on.

To make a delicious pot noodle,
A boiled egg or hot apple strudel,
There'll be lots of reliance
On amazing food science
To cook the whole jolly caboodle.

Just for a taster, try these gross and awesome food science facts as a starter:

## Yummy jelly beans and why they look so tempting...

Shellac is a chemical that is often used to improve the shine of wood and furniture. Yet it can also be used to improve the shine of some foods, such as jelly beans. Where does shellac come from? It oozes from an insect in Asia called the lac bug. Delicious! Oh yes, and those lovely red jelly beans (as well as plenty of other red-colored food) can have dye in them called cochineal. It comes from a crushed-up tree bug. Mmm.

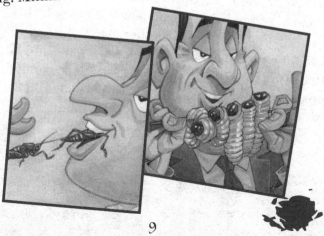

It might be best to stick to a good healthy salad. We all know that's good for us, don't we? True—but some salads might be hiding something foul if scientists have been at work. In many fast-food restaurants, packaged salads are dusted with a chemical called Propylene Glycerol to keep lettuce crispier for longer. This chemical is also used in antifreeze—so maybe eating lots of lettuce will stop you feeling frozen (unless they're iceberg lettuce!)

When scientists tested bottled water, about one-third of the samples contained synthetic organic chemicals, bacteria, and even arsenic. In a study, more than 900 bottles and 100 store brands were tested by the U.S. National Resources Defense Council of the USA. If you prefer a drink from the faucet, in some places there are more than 115,000 human-made chemicals that are finding their way into the public water supply system. So next time you pour a glass of water, you might need to water it down before you drink it!

# How about some gross AND awesome food science facts?

**1**

Many packaged processed cheeses aren't cheese at all but a "cheeselike substance." Any cheese product labeled as processed includes additives, chemicals, and flavorings that make up 49 percent of the total product. That cheap cheese in your fridge has just enough real cheese in it to allow companies to call it cheese. And as for what food technologists squeeze into some sausages... it's so disgusting, we're not allowed to tell you.

**2** Casu Marzu is a cheese made from sheep's milk with a little help from biology. Cheese flies are purposely added to the mixture. This cheese is a delicacy in Sardinia, and as it is made, the young flies and maggots go hyper. The taste of this maggoty cheese is so strong it can burn your tongue, and if the undigested fly larva get into your intestines, you'll be spending a long time in the bathroom. Enjoy!

**3** When Swiss cheese ferments, the bacteria inside creates a gas. When the gas is released, it forms bubbles in the cheesy mixture. This is how the holes are made in Swiss cheese. The great news is, you can eat as many of the cheese holes as you like and not put on any weight. That's clever cheesy science.

## Cheesy joke

Did you hear about the biologist who made his own moldy blue cheese packed with mushrooms and took it to a party? After all, he was a fungi (fun guy). Groan.

Time for some GRUB!

# WoW Science

While on the subject of mold...did you know the first antibiotics were discovered by accident? In 1928, the Scottish scientist Alexander Fleming was growing bacteria in his lab but he used a dirty petri dish by mistake. Mold began to grow in it and ZAP! It killed off the bacteria. From this mold, Fleming developed the drug Penicillin, which is now used by doctors to kill bacterial infections.

## Moldy joke

Microbiologists often travel the world and speak many languages. After all, they are people of many cultures (get it?). It's best not to let one make your lunch—just in case.

# Stinky Space Science

Would you like to be an astronaut and travel in space? Hundreds of scientists have done research in space and many have stayed for months in space stations. But it's not all cool science. There's a downside of being "up there"…read on to find out why!

My rocket salad is really taking off.

1 The Apollo 8 mission prepared the way of the eventual moon landing of Apollo 11. It was commanded by Frank Borman but Houston, he had a problem. He woke from a nap with an upset stomach. He vomited and had diarrhea, the globules of which floated all over the inside of the space craft in zero gravity. It took so much cleaning, he was spaced out—tee hee.

This problem is of great gravity (or not enough)

2 On Earth, we hardly notice our skin cells flake off, as gravity makes them fall to the ground. In space, however, there is no gravity to pull the dead cells away, so they float all over the space craft. With many astronauts living together on a Space Station at the same time, they have to cope with floating clouds of dead skin wafting all over the place. Gross.

**3** Yes, you have to ask the question, don't you? How do you go to the bathroom in space? Engineers have designed various toilets with tubes, funnels, and vacuum pumps, but more often than not, it's a matter of recycling urine so it can be drunk again and again. So if you want to fly in space, you need to be prepared to drink your own pee. Don't worry, it's totally safe. It's all good recycling (or pee-cycling).

**4** Another thing about flying in space; people get taller because there is no gravity pulling down on them. They can't burp in space as there is no gravity to separate liquid from gas in their stomachs. Farts can happen but the gas stays right there. Special filters inside astronaut suits deal with nasty human gases like methane and carbon dioxide.

# Astronomy Jokes

Q: How many ears does Captain Kirk have?
A: Three. A left ear, a right ear, and a final frontier

Q: What do you call an alien with three eyes?
A: An aliiien

Q: How do you get a baby astronaut to sleep?
A: You rocket

Q: Where do astronauts keep their sandwiches?
A: In a launch box

Q: What is a black hole?
A: Something you get in a black sock

Q: How do astronomers organize a party?
A: They planet.

# Undies-irable

According to **NASA** (National Aeronautics and Space Administration), Russian scientists have thought a lot about the problem of dirty underwear in space. That's because smelly underpants have to sit on the Space Station for months at a time. Scientists came up with a system to use bacteria for digesting the astronauts' used cotton and paper underwear. Apart from making unwanted underpants biodegrade, they think that gas made by bacteria could be used to help fuel the spacecraft. It seems research is still in progress—be prepared to blast off!

# Foul Underpants and Cheesy Socks

Another fact about underpants in space might also surprise you. Dirty underwear and toilet paper have helped to grow plants on the International Space Station. American astronaut Don Pettit discovered that by folding a pair of underpants into a sphere shape and stitching in some Russian toilet paper (which is thick, wool-like gauze), this created a warmer environment for some tomato and basil seeds to start to sprout. Like their socks, astronauts' underwear is only changed every 3 to 4 days—so he figured the underpants might provide extra nutrients for the plants. Flowers should do well—especially any bloomers!

# A Dump on the Moon

The moon is littered with trash from when Apollo astronauts walked across its surface. Everything from dirty clothes, rovers, probes, flags, and trinkets were left behind—almost 200 tons of rubbish. So if you ever go to the moon, watch where you step. Astronauts left plenty of their own bodily waste as that would have been too expensive to return to the surface of the Earth. It will never rot away on the moon. Yuck.

Bin collection is every Moonday

# Mysteries out there

Apart from our dirty moon, we have eight planets in our solar system. However, outside of our solar system there are thousands of other planets. The universe contains more than 100 billion galaxies and the largest galaxies contain a million, million stars.

Astronomers are looking for planets that may be habitable, just like the Earth. The majority of planets discovered so far are hot gas planets. But it may only be a matter of time (and space) before we will discover intelligent alien life somewhere out there.

We cannot know where in the sky
Aliens are watching, or why.
While they all keep anonymous,
It's the job of astronomers
With space telescopes to wave and shout, "Hi!"

I really fancy a chocolate Mars Bar or a Galaxy.

23

# Center of the Universe

Scientists used to get into big trouble if they suggested the Earth moved around the Sun and not the other way round. One of the first scientists to describe his ideas was a Polish astronomer called Nicholas Copernicus (1473–1543) (No, he didn't spend copper nickels). Copernicus came up with one of the first theories about planetary motion that placed the Sun at the center of our solar system, with the Earth revolving around it. Although he was right, not many people believed him.

## Joke

Copernicus' parents might deserve some of the credit for his great discovery. Apparently, when he was twelve they said to him: "Copernicus, young man, when are you going to realize that the world does NOT revolve around you?"

Next came Galileo Galilei (1564–1642), an Italian scientist who opened the eyes of the world to this new way of thinking about how our solar system works. He also invented an improved telescope so that he could gaze far into space. He was the first to see Jupiter's moons, and he also realized that our moon was full of craters. That was Earth-shattering news!

Galileo was brilliant, but despite that, his life wasn't easy. No one believed him and he was arrested, even though he turned out to be right all along. Nothing really gross happened to Galileo—except after he died. The middle finger of his right hand was cut off and put on display at the Museo Galileo in Florence, Italy—just in case you'd like to see it.

He's pointing to Jupiter!

# More cheesy space jokes

After years of detailed research, scientists have finally found what is in the very center of Jupiter. The letter "i."

A science teacher asked her students, "Which is more useful, the sun or the moon?"
After a moment, a keen student put his hand up and answered, "I think it's the moon, because the moon shines at night when you want the light, whereas the sun shines during the day when you don't need it."
Doh!

Did you hear about the astrophysicist who stayed up all night trying to work out where the sun had gone?
At last it dawned on him.

Two aerials met on a satellite, fell in love, and got married in space. The ceremony was rubbish but the reception was wonderful. The honeymoon was out of this world.

Q: Before docking with the International Space Station, what must the pilot of a space module do first?

A: That's easy—it's not rocket science. Put money in a parking meteor, of course.

# Moon Jokes

Have you heard about the new restaurant they've built on the moon? The food is great, the service is friendly, but unfortunately there's just no atmosphere.

Q: How does the moon cut his hair?
A: Eclipse it.

As some people used to believe the moon was made of cheese, how about some really cheesy cheese jokes?

Astronauts have been mining the surface of the moon and have discovered that it really is made of cheese. They've found a rich vein of brie, which they've mined twice already.
Suddenly their radio crackles:
"Mission control to cheese-base-one—we need you to get a third sample of that brie."

But the astronauts are exhausted (and cheesed-off) so they try to come up with excuses...
"It'll spoil the lunar landscape if we take too much. After all..." they all burst into song,
"Have you ever seen such a site in your life as brie mined thrice?"

Q: What's the best type of cheese to use if you're building a moon?
A: Swiss—it already has craters!

Q: Which round cheese was launched into orbit and appeared like a red moon over the Netherlands (where it is made backwards)?
A: Edam

Q: Did you hear about the cheese that failed to win a medal at the Olympics on the moon?
A: It fell at the last curdle

# Medical Science

Today's hospitals are wonders of science—with new research and techniques improving medicine all the time. But it wasn't so long ago that operations were very risky. Can you imagine what it was like for patients before they could be safely put to sleep with anesthetic? Doctors had to be super-fit to hold down screaming patients...

Surgeons back then were athletic,
Wrestling patients, they'd be energetic...
When wielding their knives,
Patients screamed for their lives
Thank science for today's anesthetic!

# Silly Hospital Sketch

Nurse: Why did you just run from the operating theater?

Patient: Because I heard a student doctor saying, "Don't be afraid—removing an appendix is quite simple."

Nurse: That's true—so what's the problem?

Patient: The student was telling the surgeon.

Nurse: I'm sure it's nothing to worry about.

Patient: Yes it is—I'm only meant to be having my tonsils out.

Nurse: Ah—that's the thing, you see. The scan showed something else.

Patient: What? What's wrong with me?

Nurse: We won't be entirely sure till the autopsy. But there could be good news.

Patient: Yes, please—give me some good news.

Nurse: You'll go down in medical science. You're about to have a disease named after you. Congratulations, Mr. Rashbottom.

# GROSS ALERT

The Scottish surgeon Robert Liston (1794–1847) was famous for being extra fast cutting off diseased limbs without using anesthetic (as well as for being big, grumpy, and scary). Only about one in every ten of his patients died on his operating table at London's University College Hospital. The surgeons at nearby St. Bartholomew's lost about one in every four. His success rate was down to speed and telling onlookers to set their watches and time him. Meanwhile, a gang of men would hold down the patient.

No need to rush—I'm reading the sports results.

In one operation to remove a leg, Liston moved so fast that he cut off his assistant's fingers and slashed a spectator's coat. The patient and the assistant both died from infections to their wounds, and the spectator was so scared that he died of shock. The incident went down as the only known surgery in history with a 300 percent death rate.

In 1846 Robert Liston made medical history. He tried using a gas called ether to put a patient to sleep. After 25 seconds, the patient's leg was removed and when he woke minutes later, he asked when the operation was going to start. Success—painless surgery at last.

It took many years for surgeons to make ether and other chemicals work properly. Sometimes patients woke up in the middle of operations and other times they died from breathing in too much gas. Sometimes the surgeon fell asleep, too. But the main killer after an operation was infection. It took another famous surgeon in London, Joseph Lister (1827–1912), to understand how bacteria infected wounds. He made sure operating theaters were made spotless and that surgeons always scrubbed their hands. Clean hospitals were ground-breaking science 150 years ago!

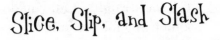

# Slice, Slip, and Slash

*The scene is the College of Surgeons, Edinburgh, in 1850. It is before anesthetics were widely used and before doctors understood bacteria and the importance of antiseptics.*

Patient: (Nervously) Can you see what the problem is, doctor?

McHackett: Yes.

Patient: This is the most scientific place for surgery in the world, isn't it?

McHackett: Yes.

Patient: This is cutting-edge modern science, isn't it?

McHackett: Yes. Definitely cutting-edge (sharpens a knife).

Patient: It's my leg, isn't it?

McHackett: Yes.

Patient: Tell me straight. Can you do something for the pain?

McHackett: I have some good news and some bad news.

Patient: Can you break it gently?

McHackett: Your leg?

Patient: No, the news. Tell me the bad news first.

McHackett: It's gangrene. Down to the bone. The leg must come off.

Patient:     Oh no. Oh no. Oh no. So what's the good news?

McHackett:  I'll give you a shilling for your boots. They're my size.

Patient:     What are you picking out of my leg with your fingers?

McHackett:  Just something I left on your wounds earlier.

Patient:     Bandages?

McHackett:  No, maggots. They did a good job eating the rotting tissue but I'm afraid I'll still have to use the knife. A scalpel for the flesh and a saw for the bone. You'll soon be back on your feet… foot.

Patient:     Tell me straight, doctor—will this really hurt?

McHackett:  No, I won't feel a thing. Besides, it's just a little saw. Get it? Just a little sore!

Patient:     But what if I scream in pain?

McHackett:  You won't.

Patient:    Really? You can stop the pain?

McHackett:  No—I'll ram a rag in your mouth.
            That will stop you screaming.

Patient:    What if I faint from fear?

I told you it might be a little saw to begin with...

**McHackett:** That might help. I just hope I won't as well. Bite on this rag when I reach the bone. I'll tie your leg tightly just above the knee to stop the blood.

**Patient:** But what if the shock kills me?

**McHackett:** You're in the best place. I can use your body for medical research.

**Patient:** I heard about something called chloroform that some surgeons are now using as an anesthetic.

**McHackett:** Not me—I need to keep wide awake for this. I'll give you a wee drop of this stuff to calm your nerves...

**Patient:** Medicine?

**McHackett:** Yes... whisky. I'll also splash a wee dram down your leg.

**Patient:** Wee down my leg? That's foul.

**McHackett:** No, whisky should stop the maggots getting frisky. And the rats. I'll pour it then call for a few young fellows to join us from the ward next door.

Patient:      This is no time for a party.

McHackett:  I'll need them to hold you down.
              It's amazing how patients wriggle,
              scream, kick, and punch when the
              knife goes in. Last week a patient
              thrashed about so much I cut off the
              wrong arm.

Patient:      The poor patient!

McHackett:  It wasn't the patient's arm I cut off.
              It was one of the helpers who got in
              the way. At least he couldn't thump
              me. Mind you, it really upset him—
              he was quite cut-up about it. Still,
              once bandaged up, he seemed fairly
              'armless.

Patient:      Tell me straight, doctor. Will you
              keep me from death's door?

McHackett:  No worries... I'll soon pull you
              through. Now bite that rag, brace
              yourself as I make the first cut.
              Quiet down, I've hardly started.
              Remember, this is the very latest
              cutting-edge science...

Patient:      But doctor... That's the
              wrong leg!
                          [FREEZE]

# Big Disease Busters

Many scientists through history have taken scary risks to study killer diseases. It is only in recent times that scientists discovered how many diseases are spread by bacteria or viruses. They once thought foul smells caused illness. Get ready for some foul science coming up...

I try to avoid this doctor like the plague.

Edward Jenner (1749–1823) was an English country doctor who changed medicine forever. For centuries, the dreaded smallpox was feared by everyone around the world. The disease spread quickly and killed millions upon millions of people. If smallpox didn't kill you, it could leave you blind or badly scarred from all the pus-filled blisters smothering your body and face.

44

Jenner noticed that farmers who caught a weak and harmless disease from cows, called cowpox, never caught the deadly smallpox. Why? He decided to put a scary idea to the test in 1796. He infected James Phelps, a young boy in his village, with cowpox by rubbing the pus from a milkmaid's blister into a cut in James's arm.

Then came the scary bit. Later he did the same with smallpox pus and scabby bits. He then waited to see if James would catch the deadly disease. He didn't!

If this works, I'll buy you a house*

*and he really did.

Edward Jenner called this "vaccination" (after the Latin for cow: "vacca"). Although many scientists at the time thought Jenner was totally foul and crazy, vaccination eventually became an important part of medicine. By injecting a weak form of a disease, the body's immune system makes antibodies to attack the real disease. So, after a lot of vaccinating around the world for almost 200 years after Jenner's experiment with James, the smallpox virus was finally declared "extinct" by 1980. Phew!

Vaccination all began with cowpox from Blossom the cow.

Stubbins Ffirth (1784–1820) was an American doctor who went far beyond the call of duty to find out about yellow fever. No one knew then that this killer tropical disease was caused by a virus spread by mosquitoes. Victims' skin can turn yellow, and they bleed from the mouth, nose, eyes, and stomach, causing black vomit.

I think I'm gonna be...

Told yer!

Seeing that yellow fever spread during the summer, but disappeared during the winter, Ffirth concluded that it couldn't be a contagious disease. He thought it must be caused by hot weather. To prove his theory, Ffirth tried to prove that however much he exposed himself to yellow fever, he wouldn't be able to catch it. He started by making small cuts on his arms and pouring "fresh black vomit" from a yellow-fever patient into his cuts...

Next he dribbled vomit in his eyes. He fried some up and breathed in the disgusting fumes then drank glasses of pure, undiluted black vomit. Still he didn't get sick—even when he covered himself in yellow fever patients' blood, saliva, sweat, and urine. He still didn't catch the disease so he declared his theory was right. Wrong! Yellow fever is very contagious but needs to get into the bloodstream, usually by a mosquito bite. Even so, it was a miracle Stubbins Ffirth didn't kill himself from his kooky science.

# Be careful what you drink

We now know that a lot of diseases can be caught by drinking dirty water where deadly bacteria can thrive. This wasn't known until scientists found out the hard way. Diseases such as cholera could soon kill many people in epidemics. They would die from vomiting and diarrhea.

In the 1850s, a British doctor named John Snow discovered that a London cholera epidemic seemed to start from a well where sewage got into the water supply.

A famous French scientist, Louis Pasteur, also agreed with this "germ theory," so he boiled liquids to kill off harmful bacteria. This was sensible science, but people then didn't think that drinking river water full of toilet waste could do any harm. Now we know.

There's nothing like a nice drop of water to flush you out.

In 1883 a German scientist, Robert Koch, discovered the exact bacteria that caused cholera. This was a great scientific breakthrough, but a rival German scientist thought this was all nonsense. He was Max von Pettenkofer (1818–1901) and he just didn't agree that bacteria in water could spread disease. He said people got sick by not washing properly or from breathing bad air. To prove his point, he publically drank a steaming cup of cholera bacteria that Robert Koch mixed up from a patient's diarrhea (pause, while you scream). After downing the cholera cocktail, Pettenkofer began to feel very weird (SURPRISE!). However, he was very lucky and escaped getting full-blown cholera. He took a dangerous risk as we now know for sure that drinking foul water can kill you.

# Forensic Science

Forensic science is the detailed study of evidence—often microscopic. The results can be used in criminal investigations or CSI (Crime Scene Investigation). This often involves collecting blood from a crime scene and analyzing it in the lab to find DNA.

Did you hear about the two blood cells that met and fell in love? Sadly it all ended in vein.

A forensic scientist reported the results of a blood test from a sample found at the crime scene.

"I have good news and bad news for the suspect. First the bad news. The blood test shows his DNA is an exact match with that found at the crime scene."

"Oh, no!" cried the suspect. "What's the good news?"

"Your cholesterol level is very healthy."

Q: What did the DNA say to the other DNA?
A: Do these genes make me look fat?

## Court Scene

Q: Are you the scientist who examined the dead body?

A: Yes, I am a pathologist.

Q: But are you qualified? Before you performed the autopsy, did you check for a pulse?

A: No.

Q: Did you check for blood pressure?

A: No.

Q: Did you check for breathing?

A: No.

Q: So, it is possible that the patient was alive when you began the autopsy?

A: Not really.

Q: How can you be so sure?

A: I could just tell.

Q: Oh, so now you're some kind of mind-reader are you? You had no scientific proof.

A: Sort of. The head was missing.

# Computer Science

Where would we be without today's amazing technology and the skills of brainy computer scientists? Unfortunately many have a reputation for being just a bit nerdy. That's a good excuse for a nerd joke...

I've been sneezing all day. Maybe I've got a virus from my laptop.

A computer scientist was walking through the forest, when he heard a little voice crying for help from behind a log. He leaned over to see a frog sitting in the mud. It looked up at him and said,
"I'm actually a beautiful princess, and if you kiss me, I'll change into my true self, and be yours forever."

Hi, I'm Lily-do you want to come back to my pad?

Silently, the scientist scooped up the frog and continued on his walk.

Soon the frog piped up again,
  "OK, buddy, maybe you didn't hear me—I said, if you kiss me, I'll turn into a gorgeous princess. What are you waiting for?"

The computer scientist ignored the frog, so it yelled from inside his pocket,
  "Hey! I'm a princess!  All you have to do is kiss me!"

Opening his pocket and peering in, the computer scientist said,
  "Listen, I spend all my time designing computer software. I don't have time for a girlfriend.  But a talking frog is just so cool."

# Crazy Scientists or Pure Geniuses?

Be warned—some of the following experiments and discoveries through history were done by scientists who took all kinds of crazy risks. Some of them seemed crazy or totally disgusting. Others dabbled in risky science or were as mad as a box of frogs. Brace yourself to meet 15 of some of the most amazing scientific minds...

This is the best way I know to make prune wine.

Archimedes was a physicist and mathematician who lived around 200 years BC. He loved science so much that sometimes he forgot to eat while he was working out problems.

We can't be sure all the stories about him are true but apparently he once boasted that he could lift the Earth if he had a large enough lever and somewhere to stand. Instead, he made a giant lever and used it to raise a ship out of the water. Then he needed to solve a problem about the weight of real gold and false gold. The answer suddenly came to him as he got in the bathtub and saw the water rise as his body displaced it. He jumped out of the tub and ran through the streets naked, shouting, "Eureka! I've got it!"

Archimedes was having a scrub
When the water spilled out of the bath
"Eureka!", all heard,
"Displacement's the word!"
And he ran in the nude down the path.

Tycho Brahe (1546–1601) was a famous Danish astronomer. His pioneering work on the movement of the planets paved the way for Sir Isaac Newton to develop the theory of gravity. As well as being a science genius, Brahe could be rather odd. In 1566 he was wounded in a duel over who was the greatest mathematician of all time. His nose was damaged for life—but his death was bizarre, too. He loved parties with a lot of drink but he had a weak bladder. Feeling it was impolite to leave the banquet table before the party was over, Brahe neglected to relieve himself before dinner. With all that drinking and not going to the bathroom, it seems his bladder burst and he died a slow agonizing death. You probably didn't want to know that.

Francis Bacon (1561–1626) was an English writer who was fascinated by science. Unfortunately, he was killed by one of his own experiments.

In 1626, Sir Francis Bacon looked outside at wintry weather and wondered if snow would preserve meat better than salt. He rushed out to get a chicken, killed it, and tried to stuff it with snow. The experiment was a failure; the chicken didn't freeze, and after spending too long out in the cold, he developed pneumonia and died. Little did he know how frozen chickens would become so popular (funnily enough, with bacon!).

**Hennig Brand (1630–1710)** was a German scientist who, like many "alchemists," believed it was possible to make gold if only you knew how. In his search for the "philosopher's stone," Brand was convinced he could make gold from that other golden substance—human urine.

Brand had a basement laboratory where he began stockpiling 1,500 gallons of urine (don't ask where he got it all). Then he set to work by boiling it down into a substance that looked like gooey honey. Eventually he ended up with white, waxy goo that glowed in the dark. He had stumbled upon the element phosphorus. The name, after all, starts with "p." Phosphorus has been used in deadly explosives, fertilizers, and for making match heads. A useful discovery and easy as pie (or pee!) when you know how.

63

Isaac Newton (1643–1727) is considered one of the most important scientists in history and is known as the "father of modern science." During his lifetime, Newton developed the theory of gravity, the laws of motion (which became the basis for physics), a new type of mathematics called calculus, and made breakthroughs in the study of light, such as the reflecting telescope. The story goes that he got his inspiration for gravity when he saw an apple fall from a tree on his farm.

That's just given me a great idea. Apple crumble for dinner!

Being interested in everything, Newton was fascinated by how his eyes worked. He even stuck a needle in his eye to see what would happen. He poked it up between his eyelid and eye and even dug around the back of his eyeball. He noted that "light and dark colored spots" appeared when he wiggled the needle around. Maybe he shouldn't have been called Isaac but Eyes-eek!

**Johann Conrad Dippel (1673–1734)** was born in Castle Frankenstein in Germany. Yes, Frankenstein. There's a clue. He became a preacher but something of a mad scientist, too. Not only did he try to make gold in his laboratory in the castle's dungeon, but he also claimed to have invented a medicine that stopped people getting old. His "Dippel's Oil" was made from blood, bones, and other body bits. In fact, it was far more useful as a blue dye.

Locals told stories of his grave-robbing at night, to use corpses in experiments—like attempting to move the soul of one body into another. Dippel's own death was strange. Some said he died of a stroke but others told of him drinking some of his own blue dye so that he would live forever. Wrong! Instead he poisoned himself, and, when found, his body had turned completely blue.

Benjamin Franklin (1706–1790) was an American politician, writer, and scientist. Among other things, he invented bifocal glasses and made discoveries about how ocean currents and winds work. He had some ideas about lightning, too—so out he went to test things... with his young son—and a kite.

The plan was to fly the kite into the storm clouds and conduct electricity down the kite string. A key was then attached near the bottom, to conduct the electricity and create a charge. Lo and behold, the kite was struck by lightning and, when Franklin moved his hand toward the key... ZAP! Sparks jumped across and he felt a massive shock, proving that lightning was huge electrical energy.

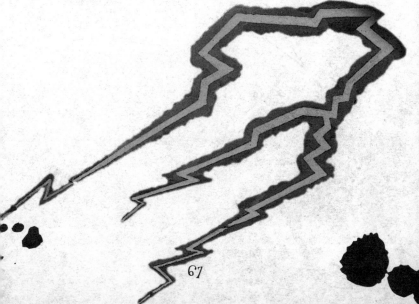

Franklin and his son were lucky to survive, as other scientists who copied this kite experiment were electrocuted and killed. But from his risky experiment, Franklin invented the lightning rod and conductor, providing the lightning with an alternative path to the earth. This proved a life-saver when lightning later struck his own house, as his lightning rod saved it from burning. Franklin's discoveries about electricity led to the invention of batteries by Volta, and the electric motor by Faraday in the early nineteenth century.

Lazzaro Spallanzani (1729–1799) was an Italian scientist with a taste for the gross—literally. He was curious about what happened to food inside our bodies, as no one knew about digestion back then. So he fed birds with food sewn inside little bags on string. After the birds had gobbled down the bags, he pulled them back out of their throats and examined the partly digested food inside. He concluded that juices in the stomach cause food to dissolve—but to make certain, he tried the same on himself.

Spallanzani sewed up bread in a small linen bag and swallowed it. Then he examined it after he went to the toilet. Although the bag was intact, the bread had gone, so he saw that acid in the stomach must be at work. Just to make certain, he ate a full meal and threw up, examined the vomit, then (wait for it) swallowed it again, only to repeat the exercise a few times. Yuck.

30 years after Spallanzini died, his crazy ideas about our stomach's digestive juices were proved to be true—by a man with a hole in his body.

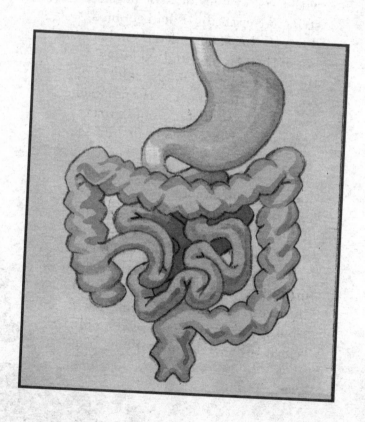

In 1822, a Canadian named Alexis St. Martin was shot and was left with a gaping hole in his chest. It was just right for army doctor William Beaumont to poke tubes through, down to the stomach. He sucked out juices to study them, as well as poked down bits of food before pulling them out again just to see what was going on. After eight years of such experiments, they learned a lot about human digestion (and yucky stomachs). Lazzaro Spallanzani would have been thrilled.

Let's do lunch.

Henry Cavendish (1731–1810) was born into a very rich family so he didn't have to worry about money. He turned his London house into a huge lab where he did experiments all day. He dressed strangely, hid himself away, and behaved eccentrically, but he made a huge contribution to science.

I'm a genius – I've discovered inflammable air.

In 1766 he discovered hydrogen and found the gas produced water when it burned. He also accurately calculated how heavy the Earth is by using a complicated machine.

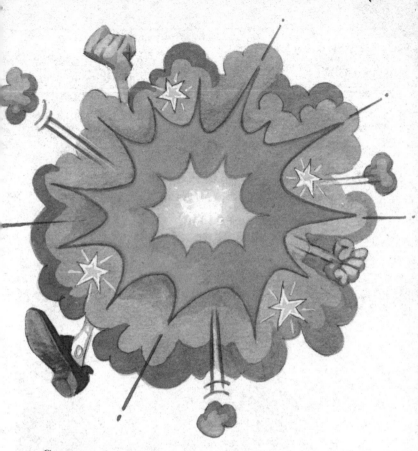

Cavendish was also fascinated by electricity and did experiments on himself. Some of his electric shocks were strong enough to knock him out. People only found out about his work from his notes after he died.

Giovanni Aldini (1762–1834) was an Italian professor of physics. His uncle, Luigi Galvani, was a scientist famous for making dead frogs' legs twitch with electricity. So Giovanni carried on the family tradition by using electricity to make dead animals wink. He wired up dead bodies to a machine called a voltaic pile, which was the first type of electric battery. Then he stopped in at the mortuary for two human heads, which he connected together with wires. When he showed people dead faces moving, they tended to faint. But then he took his show on the road to London. "Gentlemen, watch me make this freshly hanged murderer smile, wink and twitch! I just connect this wire here and hey presto…"

I'm feeling very unhoppy about this.

I'm just hanging around for the next experiment.

"The right hand was raised and clenched, and the legs and thighs were set in motion. It appeared as if the wretched man was on the eve of being restored to life."
*The London Times, 1803*

Please don't try this at home... or anywhere else.

Nikola Tesla (1856–1943) was a brilliant physicist and inventor. His ideas were way ahead of his time and continue to influence technology today. He even had the idea for Smartphone technology way back in 1901. Working for most of his life in New York and inventing hundreds of devices, he was a friendly rival to the great American inventor Thomas Edison (creator of domestic light bulbs). Some of Tesla's inventions were:

Multiphase power system for electricity (we use this today)

Wireless transmission of energy

Radar

Fluorescent light

Loudspeakers

Tesla had an amazing mind—he could speak eight languages and had the ability to memorize huge amounts of information and whole books! However, he did have his slightly batty side.

# Top 10
## Odd things about Tesla

**1** He had weird visions and hallucinations.

**2** He worked on scary "death rays."

 **3** He refused to shake hands with anyone as it "disturbed his magnetic field."

 **4** He had to wash his hands every few minutes.

 **5** He went all wobbly at the sight of fruit, jewels, pearls, or any round objects.

He would only stay in hotel rooms with numbers divisible by three.

 He always walked round a building three times before going inside.

 He freaked out if he touched human hair.

He said of a pigeon, "I love her as a man loves a woman, and she loves me."

 He spent his last years alone in a hotel room in New York (with his pigeons).

Mr Tesla is a genius pigeon fancier.

Marie Curie (1867–1937) was a Polish scientist who did important work with radioactivity, chemistry, and physics—which paved the way for discoveries like X-rays and chemotherapy.

Nothing in life is to be feared, it is only to be understood.

Marie Curie was one of the key female scientists of her day and, together with her husband Pierre, she discovered the dangerous elements polonium and radium. She died from leukemia because of the amount of radiation she exposed herself to over her career. In fact, the radiation levels she was exposed to were so powerful that her notebooks must still be kept in special lead-lined boxes to stop them contaminating people!

Albert Einstein (1879–1955) was a world-famous scientist who came up with some of the most important discoveries and theories in all of science. Some people consider him to be one of the super geniuses of the 20th century.

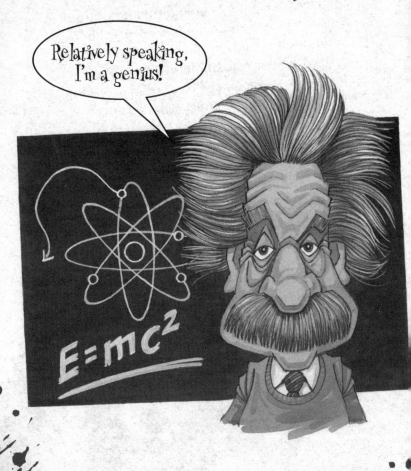

Relatively speaking, I'm a genius!

$$E = mc^2$$

Einstein's Theory of Relativity changed the way scientists look at the world. It led to inventions such as the atom bomb and nuclear energy. One equation from his theory is $E=mc^2$. In this formula, "c" is the speed of light—assumed to be the fastest speed possible in the universe. This formula explains how energy (E) is related to mass (m). The Theory of Relativity explained how time and distance may change due to the "relative" or different speed of the object and the observer—groundbreaking science.

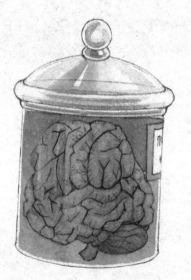

When Einstein died, the pathologist at the hospital stole his brain and sliced it up to keep in jars. What a no brainer!

# A Relativity Limerick

Doctor Einstein must surely be right;
If you traveled much faster than light
You might shoot off one day
In a Relative Way,
Returning the previous night

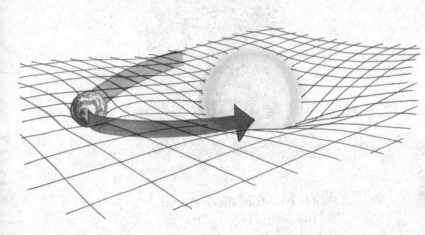

Einstein developed a theory about space... and it was about time, too.

And it's not true that Albert Einstein's brother Frank was into making a monster from body parts, either!

Thomas Midgely (1889–1944) was an American chemist who had great ideas about science, but the results were often disastrous.

**1** In 1921 he added lead to gasoline to make car engines run better. It worked fine for cars but not for people. Lead poisoning caused untold damage to people's health for decades—which is why lead-free gasoline had to be introduced.

**2** Midgely had a bright idea to make fridges work better. He added a gas called CFC which made them cool really well. Sadly, if the gas escapes, it goes straight up to the ozone layer and destroys it. This has caused serious climate change over the years and has greatly harmed our planet. Another turkey, Thomas!

3. No one realized at the time how bad for the environment Midgely's inventions were. When he became badly disabled by the disease polio, he didn't give up inventing. He designed a machine to help him move in bed but that went wrong, too. One night he got tangled up in the straps and they throttled him to death. Oops.

Erin Schrodinger (1887–1961) was a physicist who dreamed up the most famous experiment that's never been done—just to make a point. In a nutshell, this is it:

Put radioactive rocks in a box, with a radioactivity detector at one end. Add a bottle of toxic gas with a hammer suspended over it. If the detector goes off, it will release the hammer and smash the bottle. Add one cat and close the box. Now wait...

The radioactive rocks might or might not set off the detector, so the cat may or may not survive. There's no way of telling without opening the box. So Schrodinger concluded that, in theory, the cat was both dead and alive until the evidence was staring you in the face (or scratching it to bits). Make sense? Hmmm—that's quantum physics for you!

In fact, maybe it wasn't a cat in the box at all.
It might have been Mrs. Schrodinger trying to
hide from her strange husband...

# Limericks for Schrodinger's Cat

Poor Schrodinger's cat, in its prime
Got locked in a box (what a crime)
With hammer and rocks in
And virtual toxin,
Tabby was dead and alive at the same time.

*Just to make this absolutely clear:* Quantum physics tries to explain the behavior of matter and energy by understanding the nature of atomic particles (and sometimes cats).

If Schrodinger's cat had a kitten,
More physics would have to be written
To explain paradoxes
Like could identical boxes
Get unequal and potentially disproportionate
energetic hypothetical felines to fit in?

Who said science is tricky?

The cosmologist, Prof Stephen Hawking
With a computerized method of talking
Blasted squeals in a lecture
And the fault, I conjecture,
Was the ghost cat of Schrodinger
squawking.

*Yes—it was both dead and alive! (Not so much quantum physics as phantom physics?)*

# Jokes for Scientists

You might need to ask a scientist to explain some of these. If you get them all by yourself, you could either be a scientific genius or totally loopy—you decide!

## Biology

Q: What's the difference between a dog and a marine biologist?

A: One wags a tail and the other tags a whale.

Did you know... biologists have just found a gene for shyness. They would have found it earlier, but it was hiding behind a couple of other genes.

Q: Why can't you hear a pterodactyl going to the bathroom?
A: The P is silent

# Chemistry

What's the first thing you should learn in chemistry? Never lick the spoon.

Q: What do you do with dead chemists?
A: Barium

Old chemists don't die–they just fail to react.

97

I was in chemistry class today and the teacher asked me to name an element. So I stood up right in front of her and shouted "AHHHHH!"

Startled, she said, "What was that!?"

"The element of surprise," I said.

She then threw sodium chloride and an accumulator at me.

That's assault and battery!

Q: $H_2O$ is the formula for water. What is the formula for ice?
A: $H_2O$ cubed. (That's a lie!)

Our chemistry teacher asked the class, "What is the chemical formula for water?"
So I piped up, "HIJKLMNO"
The teacher asked, "Where did you get that from?"
I replied, "Yesterday you said it was H to O!" ($H_2O$)

# An alchemy limerick

A scientist peered into her beaker,
And what she saw started to freak her
In the slimy green mold
Shone a glimmer of gold
Her lost ring—a wonder of science—
EUREKA!

# Physics

Q: What's a nuclear
   physicist's favorite meal?
A: Fission chips.

Q: Why is electricity so dangerous?
A: Because it doesn't know how to
   conduct itself properly.

I read an interesting book on anti gravity, but found it difficult to put down.

Why did the physicist disconnect her doorbell? She wanted to win the no-bell prize.

A group of protesters in front of a physics lab were demonstrating:
"What do we want?"
"Time travel"
"When do we want it?"
"Yesterday. Whenever. Irrelevant."

What does a subatomic duck say? Quark!

Two atoms are walking along. One of them says:
"Oh, no, I think I lost an electron."
"Are you sure?"
"Yes, I'm positive."

Never trust atoms to tell you the truth.
They make up everything.

And now for a nerdy limerick for physicists:

Add fourteen thousand, five ninety-eight to John Hancock's signature date
Find the square root and divide by point eight.
Times it all by eleven
Then add sixty-seven,
For the year Allessandro Volta met his fate.

\* The physicist who invented the electric battery—and gave his name to volts and voltage. His ideas were truly electrifying.

Which means...

14598 + 1776 (Declaration of Independence) = 16374
The square root of 16374 is 128 (128 x 128 = 16374)
128 divided by 0.8 is 160
160 x 11 = 1760
Now add on 67 and you have the date of Volta's death: 1827
(*A physicist like Volta could probably work all that out standing on his head—so long as it was before that date!)

You need to know the symbols
of elements of the periodic
table for these cheesy jokes:

Dogs are made up of calcium,
nickel, and neon.
(CaNiNe)

| 1 H Hydrogen | | | | | | | | |
|---|---|---|---|---|---|---|---|---|
| 3 Li Lithium | 4 Be Beryllium | | | | | | | |
| 11 Na Sodium | 12 Mg Magnesium | | | | | | | |
| 19 K Potassium | 20 Ca Calcium | 21 Sc Scandium | 22 Ti Titanium | 23 V Vanadium | 24 Cr Chromium | 25 Mn Manganese | 26 Fe Iron | 27 C Co |
| 37 Rb Rubidium | 38 Sr Strontium | 39 Y Yttrium | 40 Zr Zirconium | 41 Nb Niobium | 42 Mo Molybdenum | 43 Tc Technetium | 44 Ru Ruthenium | 45 R Rho |
| 55 Cs Cealium | 56 Ba Barium | 57 La* Lanthanum | 72 Hf Hafnium | 73 Ta Tantalum | 74 W Tungsten | 75 Re Rhenium | 76 Os Osmium | 77 I Irid |
| 87 Fr Francium | 88 Ra Radium | 89 Ac** Actinium | 104 Rf Rutherfordium | 105 Db Dubnium | 106 Sg Seaborgium | 107 Bh Bohrium | 108 Hs Hassium | 10 M Meitn |

| * | 58 Ce Cerium | 59 Pr Praseodymium | 60 Nd Neodymium | 61 Pm Promethium | 62 Sm Samarium | 63 E Euro |
|---|---|---|---|---|---|---|
| ** | 90 Th Thorium | 91 Pa Protactinium | 92 U Uranium | 93 Np Neptunium | 94 Pu Plutonium | 95 A Amer |

Which fruit contains
Barium and double Sodium?
BaNaNa

OMG! Did you hear that
Oxygen and Magnesium
are a couple?

| | | | | | | 2<br>**He**<br>Helium |
|---|---|---|---|---|---|---|
| 5<br>**B**<br>Boron | 6<br>**C**<br>Carbon | 7<br>**N**<br>Nitrogen | 8<br>**O**<br>Oxygen | 9<br>**F**<br>Fluorine | | 10<br>**Ne**<br>Neon |
| 13<br>**Al**<br>Aluminium | 14<br>**Si**<br>Silicon | 15<br>**P**<br>Phosphorus | 16<br>**S**<br>Sulfur | 17<br>**Cl**<br>Chlorine | | 18<br>**Ar**<br>Argon |

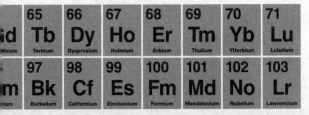

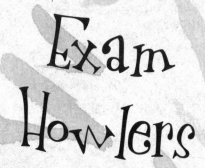

# Exam Howlers

(These answers were written to science exam questions)

Q: What is a fibula?

A: A small lie.

Q: Write two hundred thousand in figures:

A: Two hundred thousand in figures.

Q: How can you delay milk turning sour?

A: Keep it in the cow.

Q: Julian has 48 slices of cake in front of him. He eats the square root. What has he now?

A: A square mouth and diabetes.

Q: What were the first cells on Earth?

A: Lonely.

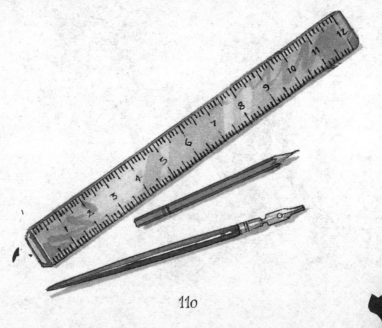

**Q:** Give a brief explanation of the meaning of the term "hard water":

**A:** Ice.

**Q:** What is the process for separating a mixture of chalk and sand?

**A:** A process called flirtation

**Q:** Where are magnets often seen?

**A:** On a dead body. I found magnets crawling all over a dead cat.

# Questions in a biology exam:

Q: Give an example of movement in plants and an animal that cannot move.

A: Carrots in a truck and a dead cat.

Q: Explain the term "germination."

A: It means to move to Germany and become a member of their nation.

Q: Name the four seasons.

A: Salt, pepper, mustard, and vinegar.

Q: Explain why mushrooms always grow in damp places.

A: Because they look like umbrellas.

If I take a photo of my blood cell, will it be a cellfie?

# And Finally...

A book about gross and awesome science wouldn't be complete without a whiff of toilet science. After all, the science of poop could help to save our planet.

"Clean" ways of making energy are major areas scientists keep exploring. As gross as it sounds, one day all our electric light could come from toilets. A daily output of one person's poop can actually power a light bulb for up to 9 hours. That's better than a chicken, which can only supply enough electricity in its lifetime to run a 100 watt bulb for 5 hours. Yet the amount of dung one cow plops in a day can power two light bulbs for 24 hours. Gas from the poop of 500 cows can power 100 homes for a day. So put the entire poop from everything together and that's mighty poop power for the whole planet!

How much energy do you need to produce an atomic bomb? A lot—but did you know that you could actually produce that amount of energy yourself? Yes, apparently scientists with nothing better to do have calculated that it's possible— but only if you constantly pass gas for 6 years and 9 months (or if everyone on Earth ripped nine farts at the same time). Amazing science—but it would hardly win the Nobel Peace Prize.

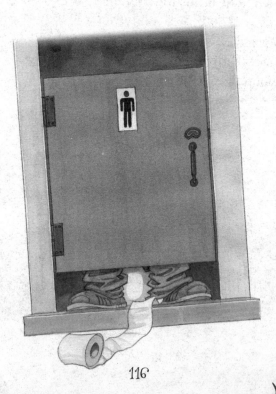

Just think… if all the data that scientists generate could be put to good use, we might solve all the world's problems. But, as someone once said, "not everything that can be counted counts, and not everything that counts can be counted." Maybe they had a good point.

Why did the germ cross the microscope? To get to the other slide!

117

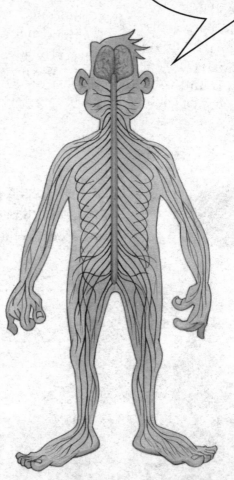

# QUIZ

1. What bug oozes a substance used in jelly beans?

a) The humbug

b) The lac bug

c) The centipede

2. How do astronauts go to the toilet in space?

a) They duck behind a crater

b) They recycle their urine so it can be drunk again and again

c) They just have to hold it in

3. Why did Galileo's theories get him in trouble?

a) He wrote a lot of rude words in his homework

b) He claimed that the world revolved around him

c) He claimed that the Earth was not at the center of the solar system

4. How did Robert Liston revolutionize medical science?

a) He developed anesthesia

b) He used extra sharp medical tools

c) He discovered several new diseases

5. Which disease did Edward Jenner infect a young boy with as part of the first vaccination?

a) Chickenpox

b) Cowpox

c) Giraffepox

## 6. How did Hennig Brand accidentally discover phosphorus?

a) He was boiling urine in an attempt to make gold

b) He was boiling gold in an attempt to make urine

c) He found it hiding under his bed

## 7. What inspired Isaac Newton's theory of gravity?

a) He saw an apple fall from a tree

b) He fell from a tree

c) Aliens told him about it

8. What is forensic science the study of?

a) Foreign sick

b) Evidence of alien life forms

c) Evidence taken from crime scenes

9. Why are Marie Curie's notebooks kept in lead-lined containers?

a) They're contaminated with harmful radiation

b) She wanted to make sure no one read her diary

c) They're so boring—no one wants to read them anyway!

## 10. What is the name of Einstein's famous theory?

a) The Theory of Nativity

b) The Theory of Festivity

c) The Theory of Relativity

**Answers:**

1 = b
2 = b
3 = c
4 = a
5 = c
6 = a
7 = a
8 = c
9 = a
10 = c

# GLOSSARY

**accumulator:** a large and rechargeable electric cell

**anesthetic:** a substance that numbs the feeling of pain.

**chemotherapy:** a cancer treatment using chemical substances to kill cancerous cells in the body.

**gene:** part of a strand of DNA. Each gene contains information that helps to define the characteristics of the plant, animal, or person to which it belongs.

**ozone layer:** a layer of ozone gas just over 6 miles above the surface of the Earth that protects the planet from much of the Sun's harmful radiation.

**radiation:** when energy is emitted in waves from unstable radioactive particles as they break down or "decay."

**telescope:** an instrument made from glass lenses that makes far away objects appear much closer.

**x-ray:** a form of electromagnetic radiation that can be used to produce pictures of the insides of objects that are invisible to the naked eye.

# INDEX

alchemy 63, 100

astronaut 15, 16–21, 30, 121

astronomy 7, 18, 22–24, 61

Bacon, Francis 62

bacteria 10, 12, 14, 19, 36–37, 43, 49, 50–51

Brahe, Tycho 61

cheese 11–13, 30–31

Curie, Marie 82–83, 124

Einstein, Albert 84–87, 125

Franklin, Benjamin 67–68

Galilei, Galileo 25–26, 121

gravity 16–17, 61, 64, 102, 123

NASA 19

Newton, Isaac 61, 64–65, 123

particles 92

poop 114–115

radioactivity 82–83, 90, 124, 126

recycling 17, 121

space: 15-17, 19–20, 22–23, 25, 28, 121

Tesla, Nikola 76–81

vaccination 46, 122

Volta, Alessandro 68, 74, 104

I finished reading this
Totally Gross & Awesome
book on:

........../........../..........